SPIT ON THE DEVIL

SPIT ON THE DEVIL

Samantha Bernstein

Mansfield Press

Printed in Canada

Library and Archives Canada Cataloguing in Publication

Bernstein, Samantha, 1981-, author
Spit on the devil / Samantha Bernstein.

Poems.
ISBN 978-1-77126-144-9 (softcover)

I. Title.

PS8603.E762S65 2017 C811'.6 C2017-902142-7

Cover Image: Shutterstock
Editing & Design: Denis De Klerck

The publication of *Spit on the Devil* has been generously supported by the Canada Council for the Arts and the Ontario Arts Council.

ONTARIO ARTS COUNCIL
CONSEIL DES ARTS DE L'ONTARIO
an Ontario government agency
un organisme du gouvernement de l'Ontario

Canada Council for the Arts
Conseil des arts du Canada

Mansfield Press Inc.
25 Mansfield Avenue, Toronto, Ontario, Canada M6J 2A9
Publisher: Denis De Klerck
www.mansfieldpress.net

For Michael,
the most reasonable optimist.

TABLE OF CONTENTS

SEASONAL POEMS

SÉANCES

"With antecedents,
With my fathers and mothers and the accumulations of past ages;
With all which, had it not been, I would not now be here, as I am..."

Walt Whitman

"In a package of minutes there is this We.
How beautiful."

Gwendolyn Brooks

SEASONAL POEMS

WINTER 2017

1

The kitchen is a mess,
the candle won't light,
it's getting late.

Two and a half minutes
to midnight,
the boys keep telling me, as though I hadn't heard
the news; hell, since Michael's prescient
piece at the end of the year,
I have visions of mushroom clouds
surging as I come (now
that's bringing work home),
and then know such annihilation
(the bombs, not the *petit mort*)
an utterness so beyond us
it serves as no deterrent—no not to life or
war, which seems the strangest part:
all existence strung on imagination,
a collectively conjured nightmare
in which enemies, *semblables,*
walk abreast through the same
nowhere.

It is good to have enough water
to wash all the dishes and take a shower, good
to be certain of trash collection. There are fifty-seven
water advisories
in this province alone.
Elected officials wish to bury
nuclear waste on the shores of Lake Huron.

2

The comedians, great moralists of our day,
are giving lessons in reality, like
literally, on the meaning of and necessity for
an objective one, as it is known. John Oliver, as text
ing teenage girl, parrots the journalist on CNN:
What does he mean when he says words? A question
we should always ask—Freedom is, after all, a mortgage
company, mobile subsidiary, arms manufacturer (owned
by Cerberus—seriously); but when this is queried of The President
of an administration that holds the people
beneath umbrellas on Inauguration Day
were protecting themselves
from the big-league heat of God's
pleasure, the laugh
catches in the throat.

Is it fair
to say we beget what we conceive? Not entirely,
for conceptions follow our acts; to know
is a moment, but all our knowledge
comes in past tense—symbol
ever the serpent's head
hungering for its tail.
The a-bomb, Michael explains, as I
wipe the counters, the thing that could contain
the horror of World War (one day of wastage in the First,
my recording angel reveals, equal to all Americans
dead from Vietnam). A comforting calculation,
this, MAD as the labyrinth humans built to hold
our immortal minotaur. Measuring violence,
my love stands zoetic, strong,
black toque against the ancestral crystal:
my young man who will
never have to leave for war, *ptu*!
spit on the devil, which is to say is protected
by accident of geographies
from being deleted

by faulty reasoning—the incurable failure
of imagination to construct from a scrap
the quilt from which it's torn.

3

And isn't that the stitch
the happy liberals dropped?
Having lost
what it feels like to feed our children
into the maw of nonsense,
its sudden gaping has us all
in a twitter, evidence our little patch
of peace was rent
imperfectly by the monster's teeth
and we like all the rest
can still be flung
arbitrarily into oblivion.

It appears the inoculation didn't take,
though so carefully prepared: those germs of information—
the corpses that could be props
for all we know
of the lives the bodies held, vignettes
of suffering delivered in leaflets—we did our duty
and consumed, the solution, alas, too weak.
The body felt but did not learn
the sickness it was party to.

The kitchen still
is not clean, waste
bin overflowing, and dinner
needs making. But I am writing
this poem. What can such an exercise
possibly be for,
except to see
inwards or towards?
Necessary, yes, but
if the latter, there are also meetings
I should right now be attending.

What is this trying to say? (As Mom would demand
of zygotic high school and undergrad essays [I have

a mom who asked, you see, part of the endowment that yields
days spent with my head
up the ass of the nineteenth century, scoping for disease
that warped our present age]).

My daughter, who cannot yet draw faces
makes maps on every scrap of paper:
to relay relation
the first function
of representation.

4

The clocks stopped
in the ice storm; when at last
I ask my phone, it's 11:11 –
reflexive superstition I wish
for existence to continue
beyond what I can envision—
proceed to the basement
with dirty laundry,
carry up what I've cleaned.

The day the nuclear priesthood
(those ministers who translate
the signs of our unknowable fate) made
their announcement about the doomsday clock,
the news ran swiftly through the currents
but no message arrived
saying where the meetings would be
to determine what to do.

Yes yes, North America, I'm writing the poem not in my right mind,
I'm *sentimental for the Wobblies,* for Noam Chomsky, for fucking 2003
when Bill O'Reilly seemed like a nutcase and one fake pretense for war
was all we had to worry about—Oh, 'twas a simpler time
in comedy! When politicians said words and the culture industry told us
what they meant!

The nice white lady Liberal
Minister of Indigenous Affairs (a post
tastefully renamed in recent years) has received
A Mandate to Negotiate. That is,
to find the Goldilocks chair
of compensation
for the thousands of children
wrenched from those who cherished them.

She talks severance
of language and tradition, says what we need
now is not just reconciliation
but reconcili*action*.
And I cannot bear to imagine
the moment of satisfaction
in the meeting that fashioned that word—Oh
yes! someone breathed over a laptop,
That really sends the message.

5

It is cold
as a monster's cave.
Ida's first simile. She is three
and a half, as she tells everyone, with perfect faith
she is the sun and all bodies spin
in her orbit (she loves planets, knows
Earth the only one life inhabits); 'til someday
the eyes of others will become stars
a thousand light years away,
and no map can chart
the space between her and them—
only the right sounds or touch, these wondrous things
the body does, can take her to them.

A deep organ is rising
from the basement, ascending
in weirdly hopeful chords, as Michael types and coughs and tries
to explain the relations of U.S. and Russia (in fast-forward
a man says *civilizational distinctness*); he clicks
and types, plays tape, and the music
grows more dissonant. (I think
how the dissident Schlegel sister hears
goblins in Beethoven's Fifth; they observe quietly,
grin: *Panic and emptiness! Panic and emptiness!*)
It's an odd time
to be writing the news, when the POTUS
calls it fake media, and his
chief strategist reports
on what never happened. It is,
the CBC tells me
a time of definitions.

In the loft in the days of our youth
my then-boyfriend used to shadow box,
and now some nights as I wash dishes
he tells me the news and once more
assumes a fighting stance—the gate,

I learn his old teacher called it: first position,
arms before the face, sprung to snap
when force tries to break through. My first association:
gate, as in that which opens.

6

It is late. I am
cleaning and talking. Are you
ever petrified, I ask, by the fact
so much depends upon
people we can't know?
This, my love replies, is why
I need the news. To make a narrative,
which is how we forgive
the world for furnishing this (his arms the gate)
when this (he opens as for
embrace) exists.

It is good
to think what words mean, good
to sweep the floors and think
some dust will miss the bin.
We cannot get it all in.
Unfinished
is different from not begun,
unfulfilled from deferred,
unsaid from unheard.

There is too much terrain
ever to traverse; even our own
selves are beyond the gate, its shadow
a black spot in our sunshine—that line
(poor panicked Carlyle, blurred with fear,
who might have seen so clearly)
comes to me tonight as Michael
shares the findings of the scholar
whom he interviewed:
conservatives dislike comedy (prefer
talk radio) because quicker to rouse
to fear; liberals, it appears, are less inclined
to rapid spikes in cortisol, find comfort
in ambiguity. And that is fine,

laughter helps us sleep (I'd never thought
why late shows are late!)—after all
the so-called leader of the free
world doesn't know how
to shake hands properly, that is, to fulfil
a basic symbolic act
of mutual recognition, and yes,
it's funny to watch him try.
I'm tired.
I'll clean the bedclothes
tomorrow.

7

It is well
to watch and weave complex
and lovely tapestries, but only if
when asked can tell what time it is,
which is to say what world
we're in, take down
minutes at the meeting and the phone number of our MP.
Is that an ugly line? Too bad. Our strategy
of late has failed. We tucked
our children in their beds, argued
vaccines and gluten free bread; in our spare time
read the news or turned to the philosophers
who strode confidently and lay
banana peels beneath the foundations
of power, ourselves included.
And irony is strong, but iron stronger;
doubt is the fair position, but it never
built a wall, or
anything at all.

During the meeting for the strike at the university, the calls of Shame
to rouse the crowd, people screaming down the mic, the argot of blame
and rage repelled me. Men in beards controlled the room, the others
fought to tell their tale or sat in silent gloom. It was tedium and confusion.
No communist picnic, this—did you know such things existed?
And summer camps and discussion groups? Grandpa Harry loved them
(Michael reminds me) in Timmins as a kid, before he learned clarinet
in the army, dentistry on the GI Bill, started a practice in Waterloo.

If we could have 1950s taxation without
the barbarous racism, women bound in aprons,
witch-hunts for queers and Commies, it would be
Utopia. There, that's the most liberal thing I'll say tonight.

8

The strike won its quixotic demands, though
of course imperfectly, and the jargon-headed god
of profit grows more arms by the day, has taught
the Academy to devour itself—at least those piquant parts
that serve the Liberal Arts (on the radio
a Dean says the answer is to court
students from former Eastern Bloc countries, who yet
value the Humanities.) At the school of higher learning
where I have spent my adult life, all the towers
look like bunkers, but we have not prepared.
We're the *New Yorker* cartoon
of the well-provisioned shelter
without a fucking can-opener.

Many of our leaders learned in school
how to duck and cover, listened when
the comforting white man said to get
ready, like Bert the Turtle, to cover their eyes:
the flash is brighter than the sun.
Even on a beautiful spring day,
these children *remember no matter*
where they go or what they do, the atom
bomb could explode right then. A flash!
They throw themselves against the walls
as if shards of glass or
toppling chalkboards
were the great danger,
and not that their flesh
will hang from them *like tattered rags.*
I learned this from *Obasan,* read it
for an English class, weeping
on the subway train on a bright spring day.
But others read it and did not weep,
or did not read and still they passed,
and my tears do less than a wooden desk
to protect me or anyone.

They call it winter, as though
annihilation were a season, but we have not learned
(though the Torch of Science burns
ever so bright) to measure just how many tonnes
of nuclear bombs will relay the fear
of destroying all life to the ones with the buttons,
yet leave an atmosphere
that might possibly foster
another spring.

9

What is buried
is not contained; it leaks
into everything, and every one
of us is downstream, though some
farther than others. For those
just feeling now the iron rods
of power that shape the earth we tread,
take heart: this is not news
and many know
how to resist. Populist
has several definitions,
pasts. Listen to those
who've been doing the work.
Go look at their maps,
stand where they ask.
Bring the children,
bring a picnic. Share.

Am I being didactic? Sorry; bad habit. You've been very patient
and I've almost done. Michael (who does not mansplain, as
we laughed recently, quite equal in dispensing pedantry) says all
the chaos these days is poking the bear, that is, the liberals who've been
cozily dreaming, waking only to grumble. When injustice isn't news but
fact for our neighbors, ourselves, co-workers'
daughters, conceptions
beget useful acts.

I do regret
it has taken this long,
know for many, the we
of this song
is beyond the gate and hasn't earned
admittance. I hope
it is not too late.

At thirty-six I've only just learned
the meaning of space: not just vastness

but utter lack of relation,
matter we can't hear, lacking a medium
through which to transmit. In our denser
atmosphere we are woven tight
as cloth, pressed close as grains
of sand that bring distant bodies
near (to magnify: this
knowledge keeps my love, imperfectly
from blindness). I had not been taught
our pores and ears
are filled with one another—relative, that is,
to the nothingness beyond.

Some things remain: *Love*
flows through the roots
of the trees by our graves;
we are mostly water,
flinch from pain.
Spring is coming—
a raw time: first struggles
are awkward, and people
apt to rhapsodize but stay indoors.

Should any seed take root in me, grow
eyes and ears, a heart, this is what I have:
there is no other time
in history, nor place,
that furnished greater odds
to learn your face
as it changes with the seasons.
The fabric is whole, if torn,
and neither the unknown nor reason
ever deterred anything
from being
born.

GREETING CARD FOR GREETING CARDS

Today I want to celebrate
The power of your art,
Your gift of speaking truly
To so many unknown hearts.

Though some may criticize your form
As mass-produced sentiment,
The commemorations you proffer
Are pleasing testaments

To the manifold loves that give
Our lives their buoyancy and light.
If we mark days in tidy rows
Of words we did not write,

And glitter or odd photographs
Give form to what we feel,
It is our fate that things this slight
Hold loves so vast and real.

And so I love the truth you speak
To the power of our will
To make our animating force
Be visible, hold still.

FOR LILY, BENEATH A FULL MOON ON THE NIGHT OF HER BIRTH

Even in the city, life obeys its own laws:
the moon conjures crocuses, though the streetlamps bear down
counterfeit, merciless day; sculptured lawns are shamed

by the supple violence of forsythia stalks; between flagstone
and fence periwinkle sprawl roughshod among the greening grass;
daffodils turn toward each other, their graceful riot

too much itself simply to be an instrument
of human vanity. You see, sweet girl, beneath
the city lays a parallel world, an ancient system that knows

nothing but to grow; the subterranean pulse of potential
existence: untraceable highways of roots; stolid bulbs that push forth
through hard earth that every year yields for them.

This night, new life spills into the streets like a revolution,
a kaleidoscopic reminder of its own force; tonight
the city is superimposed, a clumsy, provisional domination.

The logic of streets, lights, homes, this moon exposes as a cheap lie,
mannequins flaunting the gauzy needs of humanity, who cannot help
but mistake stasis for order, as though death, gestation, the impervious

births of every living thing are chaos. Furled, germinal being,
never desire that life be rational, nor without opposition. Know
instead its fierce insistence, believe in existence because it is

what living things want.

GREAT MUG FIND

The second warm day of spring. Winter was so long
this year my hands aged, the skin going slack;
my fingers ripple the knuckles
like wind shivers lake. That might be cold or time
plunged in water, balancing my slippery sweetness
as she learned her limbs, kissed her duck, trickled
lake through her fingers. Hands turn to paper,
to parched mud, I want to become
as old as the folks whose mugs I took home today:
brown and cream, rounded bodies like fat teardrops,
they sat unseen amid odd bowls and glasses, leavings
from a contents sale on College St.; Michelle
as we passed said, We've been in there (seeking treasures
with Anna for their new abode), and strode west
toward The Common, where babies zoomed trucks and grown-ups
sat on pews against rough white walls; on our way back
in blue shadow we stopped, and cheered the mugs' uncanny rhyme
with those we'd found an earlier time, at the curb of a different house—
Michael and I have the one remaining, love it best. Over these new ones
we wavered, stamped as they are with a fruit bouquet and Florida, which
to me conjures my lost great aunt, Stand-your-ground, swamp, white blaze
of West Palm; but for the couple inside their house, at the end
of the day they watched their possessions disappear with strangers—
souvenirs, I presume. Some harried or joyous or calm
moment of choice. Memories I'll make up.
The wife has Alzheimer's, Michelle said, the husband
her caregiver but now needing help; he sat quietly on the porch
while two daughters managed the sale. I know that white-knuckled
competence, near elation, of surging through a day as merchant
of one's own past, divesting meanings. Quelled the sickness
I felt for them and for myself tossed in this gale
that blows seasons one after the other so fast whole languages
blossom in a day. I bowed to the shaded house,
said, I shall think of you, thank you;
our bounty resting in the stroller we pushed into sunshine.

Less perfectly aesthetic than our earlier finds,
these will make me love, I said, the marriage of beauty and ugliness—
very grand, I know, but one needs small vessels to hold
big fears. The wish
to live long enough
to see a perfect spring day
when everything is being born
except us.

FLORENCE, FALL AND SPRING

How Florence can work a jagged March day:
from lowering air, pulled steel-wool sky a cashmere shawl
strung behind campfire hair, coruscation tonguing
unforeseeable paths from her regal head. She calls
from the last of our city's payphones in one cloudless
moment to nose me outside like a pup does an old shoe, steers
infant with one long hand, sipping coffee from the other; My Duchess
of Curiosity at twenty-eight, attending court with sturdy grace.
Firenze, the world has always had your ear—
some days wrenched you by its delicate skin, but never effaced
your desire to know. To create from fear
and resilience a palace of experience. Tonight
your child is sick, husband tired; the October
twilight swallows your form, but leaves your laughter.

EPITHALAMION

Create, you say; Don't worry
about perfect. You champion the beauty
of trying—the loon's long splash forward
that may or may not lift toward
flight. Love too needs space
to flail and find grace:
your years of courtship
not wobble but dance,
making up the steps
wooing balance and chance.

Weddings for women such as us
not contracts, not security
against spinsterhood or anomie:
instead the honour and the onus
to marry in celebration
of the brave, constant work of creation.
Today, a feast for lovers who embrace
the mess and joy of possibility,
who have the vision and bravery
to map your desires and give them chase.

ON THE DEATH OF MY FATHER

Needing badly to pee
I speak to your eldest child
forestalling a history

I'd rather not know.
The shredded loyalties,
twisted loves,

the fierce proprietary
instincts, desire
for closeness

through words like
cremation, executor,
ceremony.

The conference call:
my mother, an old friend, formalities
of regret and sadness.

Today, engagement
ring a new solid weight
on my finger,

the authority
of ceremony, the modern
rituals

of death. Hours
away, your body finally
empty, we speak

of what is to be done.
And this is how we learn:
seamlessly, unceremoniously,

pick up phones, say
the correct phrases, become
acquainted with procedures.

Irving, soon enough
I will be old. And I will
know what to do

in other deaths, other
moments in need of ritual.
Therefore Father rest easy,

you have done
what any good patriarch should:
initiate me into the customs of my tribe.

AS I WAS WALKING FROM BETH TZEDEC

Outside the synagogue, the Forest Hill
Yom Kippur traffic havoc on Bathurst,
amid men with frayed prayer-books and kippas,
slim pampered wives, their daughters in Prada
whose preciousness frightens me, I realized
this walk to our car, after the shofar,
is September ending, marks a season's
change. I wanted for you, love, my tall goy,
to see where I grew up, so you could know
how come I loathed it, and it me, and how
apart from it I felt, and was. Instead
a sudden joy, as though we were children
sharing important secrets, and simply
your knowing made the knowledge beautiful.

TO THE ALLEN EXPRESSWAY

You hold for me the
fascination
                    of a vein
I've watched protrude
through years of use:
                    a stain
of existence, physical
history, continuous.
                    The rust
takes your low guardrails
in the urban version of a
                    tree planted
at my birth: decay
the unnoticed measure,
                    the growing
body tracking the course
of my life.
                    Familiarity
more vital than beauty
or repulsion,
                    the tender
artery between hatred
and devotion.

SONNETS FOR THE FLOWER-MEN

The first came to our table as we supped
on dumplings to celebrate one year wed.
Middle-aged, from someplace warm, he shuffled
through with his bouquet, above which hungry,
gentle eyes proposed gifts, husband to wife:
a rose? We smiled, shook our heads no. He passed
a second time; my darling noted how
I trailed the man's stooped frame and shabby suit
(trying not to cry: that left arm held out,
flowers cradled in the right, like something
precious, as he bent toward unseeing
patrons). The price was absurd, but my man
paid; the vendor gave us a fond look, said
Thank you, you are the first; and gave us two.

The other was young, a quiet smile fixed
above a slight body, which wore its long
hours and cheap black suit as though no other
option existed, and without umbrage.
Trumpet-cries, smoke and talk drifted above
Kensington and this lone boy offering
lights twined to the stems of frozen roses.
He passed unseen or refused through streetlit
dancers and groups of young friends, yet he seemed
sure the night would have use for him: to hawk
flowers is a job, therefore a service.
He humbly offered romance, having not
walked long enough to know our desolate
raw crossroads of sentiment and commerce.

TO TORONTO

I must love you quietly, embarrassed
by your bleak unwieldy sprawl, your cold heart
and shameless lack of fashion sense; deliberately love
what you have cobbled together so carelessly on gridded
streets predictable as a sit-com, the 1980s
a garish tattoo on your nether-regions.
Had you been born beautiful, a sultry New Orleans,
gamine Paris or majestic Damascus; were you known
for romance or elegance, or like Montreal praised
for joie de vivre; would you be less careless with your history,
wear it to advantage like other cities; had you
a compelling air of heartbreak and decadence like Berlin,
would you be something
to write about? As it is
I, at least, am yours, have spent a lifetime learning to know you, skittish
mongrel, ambitious tart: I stow my heart in Kensington
Market; in your warm red bricks; beneath the Danforth Bridge;
hoping time will treat you kindly and my
devotion isn't worthless.

LESSONS ON OPTIMISM

I

the light
    changes before I can reach my change
            he steps back to let the cars charge north

makes me wonder
    do people ever fling their offerings or

with some compunction
    give only when they have time to place it in his hand

he has
    happy faces on his cardboard sign

black magic
        marker in two circumferences of pleading

crooked reminders we
like those down on their luck to beg with pluck intact

II

exiled
            in Etobicoke I take lunch alone at a Tim Horton's
                        with the diluted sun and a perfect view of Islington
the old
        couple at the brown plastic table in the middle
of all
        the other brown plastic tables
eat their soup
they have
        the combo with coffee and sandwich looking contentedly at
each other
their pants are pressed
                                    they are not silent

III

Moon River drifting
down College St.
Bob whistling in his clean beige raincoat
always perfectly on key he used to play piano

for years Bob has been
terrific wishing gravelly goodnights
asking so politely, smiling
looking you in the eye a real gentleman
whistling and insisting
jovially that he is sober
tonight he says I'm
plastered he says
I'm terrible no
I'm terrific
terrific he promises the Johnny Cash song
he always promises
waves his thin arms
drops his lollipop hollering
you can call me anything but don't call me Sam
Bob says I'm plastered but at least I'm honest

CAPITALISM I PRAISE YOU

for your neverending ability
to convert yourself

for the peace of mind
you've provided rich and poor alike

for the sense of hope
you bestow upon hungry adolescent nations

whose most shining
aspiration is the attainment of your virtues

I salute you
for so valiantly defending inequality

for upholding
Aristotelian ideals and making modern

Social Darwinism
in all its astounding convenience

I praise you
for deliverance from the gates

of Communist
delusion and for freedom from expression

as my best
wishes can be bought for $3.95 from the drugstore

I thank you
for Adidas in Addis Ababa and the assurance

that my wealth
was earned and deserved, and also

for the knowledge
that my life demands Lysol

I thank you
for dethroned kings and disinfected serfs

for cleverly
doing things with my money I'd never think of

and also for
multiplex movietheaters and the dream

that some day
I too will purchase the beautiful housecarbaby

and own my very own life.

OLGA

As though the world were built to give her
plums, she takes my proffered fruit without
a thankyou. Hip phrases slip from her pretty
little lips melodious and noncommittal as water
over myriad pebbles, a pleasant, transparent babble.
The firm familiar roundness of her East European arms
a vulnerable pink against the bold corporate green apron
she greets and serves with a sweetness that betrays her
indifferent cute-bummed shuffle and dark eye-liner
in the early mornings. Her nights are all packed New Wave
and Britpop dances, a constellation of sleek babyfaces in expensive
haircuts living it up, making the downtown scene, freed for a few
hours from bitchy customers, dirty tables and lame corporate bosses,
Olga and all the Olgas drunk on youth, cheap
beer and the desperate importance of whatever
newest sound or style. Yet she hungers to marry young, to settle down:
I see her giving her kohl-lined brown eyes to the pampered College St.
hipster guys she fled the dead satellite of Oakville to find.
Twenty years old, sexy and cold, Olga with her studded belt and sharp
little teeth is every shopgirl since cities began: supple limbs proficient
behind lunch counters, retail counters, single girls dream Cinderella
romances as they perform their routines, youth their temporary dowry,
boredom, strange hours and cigarettes not yet etched into their tender
mouths. Now, midnight's slick streetlit gleam sweet-talks Olga's careful
deadpan face; naked it radiates expectation, she's bright with the sheen
of her nascent escape from traditional parents, from grey six-lane roads
with puffy young mothers, plastic malls and hair-gelled teenagers in
parking-lot brawls. No, there will be no multiplex blockbuster dates
for Olga, no hockey barbeques in suburban backyards.
What will the world offer to Olga? I try not to regret
the loss of my almost-ripe plum, the pleasure expected
from its sharp cold wet on my tongue, watch
her hungry, dispassionate bite.

RUMMY

Cards make us showy—I watched
the boys playing poker once,
their hands splayed like magicians'
conjuring each their special power,
and laughed down my sleeve
at their sudden swagger;
but notice now the velvety sweep
of my arm gathering cards
for Rummy on the dark porch,
the confidant shuffle and dole,
as though the raised fan obscures
what the mind well knows,
lets the body revel
in its sensation of mastery—
pull fate from the arbitrary.

2008

Now is the age
of panic on the floor,
Michael quiet and watching.

Of mornings peaceful with coffee and books until
the daycare babies come bawling at ten, swearing silently at them,
feeling monstrous. Mornings
bursting from the apartment, him and me
separately, always;

Michael I imagine flings himself down the steps limber
and unseeing onto the train, brain churning body counts,
tactics, available information

while my self goes hurtling wide-eyed towards
terror, rage or bliss there's no telling: will the city
swallow me or I it?

Tonight I saw a tree and imagined its roots,
branches inverse beneath the concrete,
imagined that concrete gone, exploded

and houses, limbs and belongings strewn over the blasted street,
imagined those roots jutting out into nothing, sucking only the unliving air
and thought not here; how lucky not here. How dare I cower
above a street certain to be tomorrow as it is today?

Now is an age like every age:
it is good to think of the pain of others,
it is wrong to make stories of strangers.
I cannot tell need from indulgence,
empathy from injustice.

Michael said everyone seems ravaged, and I thought
poor darling, he's only seeing it now.

A LIBERAL CHRISTMAS CAROL

Half a year of booze bottles
clanging in the trunk—
fifteen dollars' worth at least—
the radio tells me "a woman
police are calling an escort
was robbed and sexually assaulted
by four men in the city's west end."
Someplace I couldn't find on a map.
In the snug cell of my car
I imagine her fear,
the knowledge, This is happening.

At the beer store, I arrange my bounty
beside a woman counting crushed cans
from a buggy. Don't touch, she says to a man
pushing ahead in line; I've worked too hard for them.
Curtly, the cashier asks the woman to move
so other customers can be served.
I'm in a bit of a hurry—
Go ahead, the woman says, not looking at
me—If you'd do me the favour
Of taking these...

It was a pathetic wrestle: pin money, or a cork
for my bleeding heart, my heart
so valued and full,
the steady pump that can do nothing
but circulate its own blood.

WHAT WORTH WORDS

Remember the Tasmanian miner
who, buried for fourteen April days
in a collapsed gold mine, death
close as the quartz slab sealed
like a coffin lid above him,
found a piece of coal and composed
a letter to his loved ones on his hardened body.

(Never mind how after the dramatic rescue
the hazardous mine closed in scandal,
the reporters departed,
the whole town headed for the dole,
the news channels waged frenzied war for the miner's story,
the winner paid the miner a million dollars,
which he took with his family and left town.)

By November there was a book.

INDUSTRIAL EVOLUTION

The sun was a honey-spill
spreading across floorboards
you recently finished.

I slept right there, you said
pointing to the bare wood beneath
the window, with poplar trees
and Toshiba neon sign beyond

where noble highway overpasses
curling like thick grey smoke
enfold the fragile sky
above abandoned factory lots.

Four days with no furniture, you said,
I loved it.
The open space made me feel at home.

One grizzled beige suede chair now
rests where you slept,
the whole space swept clean
of silent huge machinery

and damp nights with lightless squatters.
Valley weeds sweeten the dusk
and you can drum then, bothering no one.

ZEES

I wanted to savage our delicate breath,
brand it, mock it with cigarettes,
a deranged wife
maiming and claiming, as if
damage could toughen, like scar tissue, stiffen
the flimsy filaments from which life is strung.
'Zees' means sweet in my ancestral tongue,
famous for imprecations,
complaints and endearments.
Zees, our familiar, named for the readiness
of his silken purr,
freshly laid to rest, blessed
with the humane end
given non-human friends.
Not ancient; suddenly gone.
Thus among the graves
near our lovely home I smoke and fume,
until my husband with his better grace
says a world that will
make such a sweet face
is worth loving.
You don't punish life, my dear one says, because
death slips its harness.

May: the venerable chestnut tree
dropping blossoms, each one
a synecdoche for its lost parent.
Kneeling, I gather
their sugary domes,
browning at the tips.
The last tombstone
we pass on our way
out of Prospect Cemetery
is for the family Candy.

HAPPINESS

We return to our familiar hurts, habitual
places sought out like the dark corners
of our childhoods: the sensual pull

of solitude in basement closets; or the shivery succor
savored beneath old, low pine boughs at the far end
of a yard, voices of dear ones drifting

across a half-cloudy afternoon, their words
a sea whose distant constancy
isolates, amplifies the rhythmic give

and take of one's own breath.
Yes, our familiar haunts, our known steady
tread in the dark alley off any crowded street

alluring as those certain small, recurring
disappointments, in the day, yourself, worst
in one you love. Desire,

the lack of something an aching reminder
that we live, have our own apodictical
wants. Then, too, the opera of arguments:

dressed in our chosen wound, we rage
festooned and glorious, staging a practiced score;
with the passionate boom and thrill of breath

hitting air, our characters bear out their tales, form
the illusion of movement. There is the visceral
pull of learned melodies, the safety

of a beat already agreed upon: gilded
in the blinding spotlight of our perceptions
we can play out a whole, brief world

at our will, brazen against the darkness beyond
the stage's lip. It is not joy, not beauty, but there is
the splendor of order. This turbulent stasis

drowns out the awesome flood of life
outside the theater door, the volatile ocean
of circumstance where action is constant

and vital though made as we navigate blind,
moved by noumenal currents, drenched
in choice and consequence.

We cannot find our steps nor the singular
tide of our own breath, there is only
the vast unseeing world to hold us.

Within this teeming emptiness our besieged vessel may
light upon a passage; drawn toward ourselves
like mouths into a first kiss, we choose and do not choose

happiness, wordless as first visions of sun and cloud
or being danced around a living room,
motion and sound focused

in the warm body that holds you.

THE FIRST MONTH

There was no fear.
Only the recurrent
worry of dropping her
over the bannister
when walking from room to room.

Worse it was as though
my body shed,
flushed with the blood
that poured from me
now we were two,

though barely—
but my body knew,
as if knowing was bearing its first bloom,
her intricately alive, her own
sure pattern.

Sometimes
I wish to yield
a child a year
for that one moon's bright clarity.

TOOTH

The first hurt
I can't soothe.
Worse:
this small bone
insisting on air,
its ache and itch
is the forebear
of every breach
in what is
that gives might
and will,
each hard need
that yields skill.
For now I can seal the rift
between you and beyond;
my finger in your soft mouth
is to you your body,
which you do not know
will soon pierce itself
with your first tool
for making the strange, delicious world
digestible.

SONG FOR IDA

Beneath gathering clouds on an August evening I sing
Ray, a drop of golden sun, Me, a name I call myself,
and you harnessed in the backseat call for more;
the post-war houses are solid and quiet. I know their clean smell,
can tell by the quality of light they shed their durable furnishings,
the food in their kitchens; these are good enough traces
of childhood. In the dark I sing and sing
this orderly progression,
drive the straight streets beneath well-grown trees,
the ones I almost ran beneath. *La,*
a note to follow so, we cross
the Allen, that artery and division; I think
our route is in you now, and someday you'll know, but tonight I can
sew up the world for you in a little song
children sang before the soldiers came—
myself you belt, a word you're sure of, *Fa*
my voice plain and strong climbing
the scale, tipping toward joy because I sing for you.

POMEGRANATE

Seeds the size of your fingernails tinkle
into the waiting bowl; juice brighter than
blood a glistening river through your fingers
as they tickle with quick joy each revealed
cluster, which does not huddle like migrants
in the bottom of a possible boat;
that is not explosive; is prototype,
this fertile shell, this life-bomb. How to tell
you, my sticky-dimpled, straight-standing love,
what your forbearers are capable of,
feed you the fatal seeds that will bind you
to a world where I cannot protect you?
Where children in Kos lie on the cold beach,
and your parents read the news, donate, keen.

SÉANCES

FOR JOE WHEN WE WERE

Twenty:
a held breath—
Pollock's paint
between brush and canvas.

EULOGY FOR FINN

They found you hanging
by a tie
of course.
Your cat, known for its tragic wail
on rare occasions when you were away,
did not give your body up but was discovered
half-starved, staring in mute horror at your form.

Your form, all bone and sinew,
too heavy to float, washed up
on a shore in Georgian Bay in spring.

On a shore in Georgian Bay in summer
you drank beer while a gorgeous girl
rubbed lotion on a brown shoulder
and life was perfect.

They found you curled in a closet
jutting bone, eyes a calm stare and decided
you'd just been in there and wasted away, though bowls of food
for the cat adorned the fetid apartment.

You were done
you said, done,
shoving stew
into your beautiful mouth.

Wait a few years, said I; you are too young.
We sat knee to knee at the table; I observed you, rapt, horrified
at the strength of my appetite.

I always picture you in the shower
with your girl, her black hair against pale grubby tiles,
face to face with you; I
feel the moment as an inhalation

after that she's shouting at you again, or materializing

on the blanket next to you at the crowded beach:
it's fate, you say, and truly
it's hard not to believe you.

She's everywhere, there's no escape, and anyway it's your luck.
She looks down and finds fifty bucks where you
you get gum stuck to new shoes, grease on sweaters received
as presents; she won thousands in the lotto and bought you pizza. And yet
that winter you found the baby pigeon outside your building,
brought it a box and placed it there,
when it died anyway,
she understood why
you told that story so many times.

So they found you outside her east-end diner, frozen and smiling
like Sam McGee. He was done, I told them;
he was tired.

Don't write me, you said, or at least no names. I agreed but really
if Finn were Dean, David, Sean or John would it matter?
When they found you on the battlefield you looked like everyone else there.

FOREVER 21

The white Lincoln Crossover stopped beside
us dangles from gleaming ledge a bronzed limb
embedded with skulls—not the cutesy ones
that dance on onesies now, but crowns of dead
humans clustered pell-mell, relic of trench
and plague gaping from exsiccated
skin. I had to wonder who he'd been
when he buried corpses in his bicep
and if the driver thinks much of the grave
now borne so smoothly through the bright hot day.

HIGH SCHOOL CHOIR DIRECTOR

We made fun of you, of course,
of your thick voice, and how when you said focus
it came out fuckus—funny corollary to your beautiful Polish face.

You were middle-aged, just,
the lines that framed your squat round nose
like impudent relatives
entrenched, divulging domestic secrets. While naively
your wide grey eyes beseeched us,
fuckus, stand straight;
and the choir would steal sly looks,
breathe, concentrate.

I thought of you tonight on my accustomed tour
of neighborhood alleys, as I drew myself up
—the habitual fill and lift of my torso
physical pleasure and brisk nod hello
to the aged woman I hope to be—
remembered you standing before the choir, full
upper lip raised in half-ironic loving smile,
arms outstretched
counting time.

You once
told us girls to stand on tiptoe
while waiting in lines
to strengthen the calves.
Sometimes, as I wipe my grandmother's ass
I feel the lesson you gave us,
that to live with grace one must find
some beauty in the disharmonious.

INDUSTRIAL EVOLUTION (A REPRISE)

1

The slow, sad days of your leaving: the knowledge
that soon it shall all be complete, and winter's pigeon-coloured sky,
        released from the concrete blocks of this old warehouse, will
no longer hover above the rustling grove of poplar trees that shimmer
on the margin
of the gravel factory lot beside the rusted CP bridge
        to alight on this black ash and book strewn desk, at whose
                centre sits the monitor and its memory: command
station, receptacle of megabytes worth of perspectives on life
lovingly collected and created by the dwellers of this home. The rooms
will be emptied, walls abolished. Every joint you joined,
        every board supported by your small, resilient frame,
        the honey-coloured floor you tore up decayed linoleum for, all
will be razed, become nameless relations
to abandoned bedframes, filthy toys, the refuse of millions.
        No eyes then
        will praise this graying light, this bleak, muddy
                beautiful view. This scene
will be committed to the private dream of history: mine, yours,
some few others whose days were framed by this eaten, fissured wood,
these rattling panes, a lifetime older than us.

2

Who else, I wonder, wanders these rooms? Maybe
some rough, unlucky woman who crashed
beneath the red neon Toshiba sign
shining through the grimy window decades ago.
Or some old, old man whose hand gripped the wooden banister
each morning the years he fought the Second World War
from between these walls,
maybe wishing the grinding machinery of his days was something more
                                        perilous, brave,
or maybe content in this sunny room, marking time by the train whistle,
punching his hours in and out, industry clanging in the busy yard below;
happy to spend lunch hours smoking at the stainless steel Canary bar,
                                        cold beer and a newspaper
whistling back through the wide streets and narrow bridges
        of the city's south-east end. And then
        there is you and I
my first time in that room, the ludicrous youth of our joined bodies,
the only way we knew to say hello, that neon glow a seedy aphrodisiac
through the uncovered window.
        We were seventeen:
what did it mean then, that urban gleam, my memory's body
leaning into your taut back that day beneath the Gardiner overpass,
motorcycle fumes our alms to the sun as we
                raced east toward your strange, your only home?

3

I was captivated by your unnatural freedom,
by the high, bare space that contained your days,
each detail of your home's history and construction,
the point in the wall that had briefly
        been one with your thumb. Drums
and bike your only possessions, those and a brain that could microscope
the cells of bureaucracy into a ramshackle structure, ragged and permeable.
        Your life, Ty, was a Byzantine city,
full of dark corners, sudden beauty, unbreachable histories; you were only
a savvy urchin in the complicated streets, scamming passage through the
lairs of Privilege. Such a maze
of a quest: forms, requests, debt, tests, dreams wheedled down
to official statements of purpose, only to begin to become someone
        who may someday know
Medicine. North star, this distant quivering constant in your cluttered sky
was navigation through the noumenal paths of your desires,
guided you again and again to the same
        hidden warehouse of your own will
where I could find you soldered to the beige couch, laptop welded to your
thighs, punching out the clackety-clack of your accidental ascension
at least one social class; your school peers a motley parade of comfortable
kids with comfortable brains,
none of whom ever gave a stoned anatomy lecture
while making gourmet salad dressing or hauling drums up rickety stairs.
        But you did, so many times
        they quiver before me, a kaleidoscope, a honeycomb
of mornings and nights nestled at home
in the belly of the city. My lover and yours
your roommates, after dinner was all joints, David Attenborough films,
Tom Waits, *Futurama* and debates: science, politics, art, philosophy
                                        the various axes around which we spun
in a chaotic kind of unison; our lives dreamed-up and seriously played
as any children's secret treehouse game.

Beyond our nest downtown's sleek towers were impervious
grown-ups: distant, unheeded, their stoic industrious bustling an
admonition at which we giggled
                                                            invisible and proud,
their vertical lives etched like roads into our minds'
maps of places we would never go.

4

Now, having left Toronto, flown in fact so east it's west,
where you have your stethoscope and white coat at last,
you come visit me on the Bayview Extension we used to delight in
chicaning down yelling over wind and CBC;
I find again our nocturnal glee speeding beneath the Danforth Bridge
lit by the night's last train or silent and steadily bearing its suicide
blockade that looked to us below like rows of luminous crosses;
and passing the shuttered Brickworks, where men now dead
made the red bricks that in my husband's dreams mean home,
I see the shades of you and me at seventeen
scrambling up the embankment there,
in morning's first hours
with no fear of slipping or being
caught.

5

Like so many urban children of the late-industrial age, decay for us was
aesthetic pleasure, refuge from the raw world of progress.
          To us, a crumbling overpass
or forsaken dockyard behind chainlink fence speaks disproven but
beautiful Ginsberg dreams, benzedrine revelations in a nation full of
promises and diners where truckers eat cherry pie and smoke cigarettes,
talk to a buxom waitress named Dolores;
a world where romantic kids could for the first time love
rooftops at dawn and alleyways, embrace grit without wincing at the cliché.
          Knowing it had all been done before,
did not destroy the sweetness of our nighttime communal ablutions
          in the vast bathroom with the rust-coloured floors, nor the beauty
of climbing the wooden ladder at night to the platform that hid
Michael's old, hard bed beneath the sloping white roof.
For there waited the tousled, long-limbed boy I love,
          and love binds us to this old, used world
          and all its told stories
          yet makes everything new.

On that ladder, water cupped in one hand,
I knew gratitude:
Toshiba sign a brief splash on my thighs in the blue city light
streaking beneath and between the stuck, dirty blinds,
I gave thanks
for the joy of my sturdy frame balancing upwards, this treacherous course
memorized over so many nights;
for these solid bones, muscles' complicity with my desires.
Young skin bared to the luminous blue, to these drafty concrete blocks,
their dust and epic spider's webs, I gave thanks
for these brief supple years reaching for sleep framed by breached
wooden casings and reflected in wavering panes
full of the dark quiet Valley.
          My friend,
disentangling your phone cord was more difficult than expected:
reckoning with the abandoned nest
          of your electrical necessities, their dusty wires a complex tribute
to how much of your life was spent in this room, to early mornings

pulsing a broken dial tone as you ignored messages
and began calls on speakerphone,
your administrative complexities bleeding through the drywall at 8am.
The cord was stuck between two others,
I had to unplug, replug, and the raw cut on my thumb
bestowed by J.R. as we packed your drums
        made every tiny push,
        every connection
        and disconnection
        hurt.
You were gone then, the day had grown
older than us, morning
stomachache jitters and sheen of no sleep, suspended tears, the tense gestation
of February rain an ancient memory, severed
        by the replay again and again of your face telling me not to cry
at the check-in desk, your eyes
        older than anything, the goodbye in them a trapped Atlantic,
        a whole history of frightened boys before vast voyages.
Raised-browed vulnerable huckster you weren't fooling me,
the world then like a tramp's coat seemed too large around you.

6

As the city did that night after our last gig, drum-haul done one final time,
instruments a sleeping band of strange animals
in the desert of the deconstructed room.
        Morning I had opened the whole space to the winter sun,
as perhaps nobody had ever done since the factories closed:
it didn't matter who saw us now, precautions needless for one final month,
fake business license unstuck from the wall, no more careful shams
for the city's inspections when we would in two days transform home
into recording studio replete with defunct machines
borrowed from Long & McQuade.
For these last days, all blinds on the six-foot windows facing east and west
were raised, blinds that for years shielded our sweet illegal domesticity
from the ad-agency hipsters and movie production crews we'd pass each
workday morning, suspiciously fresh
with our wet, unruly heads, knapsacks flung on one shoulder.

That night your home felt imperiled, exposed,
                a nest in a denuded tree,
                high rise lights a predatory glimmer in the near distance.
        The city was marching toward us through the brittle night,
        and the old concrete seemed much older, as though it might shatter
                in the rawness of this winter air,
                the brutal clarity of the coming year.

7

The room not as it was those first months, spacious, settled in itself
as an old man who knows what he's seen, waiting for summer's tender
dusk to drift through his quiet shadows; now the high black ceiling
seemed a dark space above an empty stage, the final show
packed away. Though behind my eyes a recurring image,
a body in free-fall toward inevitable earth, arms and legs flailing
a useless resistance, we packed and laughed, took photographs with
January a filtered silver through the naked panes:
bathed in this strange light, each of us glows like a visiting angel
on a daytime TV show, and seem as staged.

The men speeding toward unknown lands, like stereotypes
Michelle and I cleaned, put lives in order,
her long, competent fingers prepared gracefully for tomorrow;
the city's eviction notice, maps for the Don Valley Reconstruction
buried beneath important forms, plates,
          passports on the old teak table.
Eastern Avenue will become a berm, an artificial hill
to guard new downtown condos when the Don River floods every 150 years.

Poised on the frontier of our adult lives,
          aided by an absurd confluence of long-expected events,
          I knew this goodbye was kind compared to farewells said
          throughout centuries, final glances of homes and homelands,
                    everything known relinquished.
Such a gentle displacement, this, in the face of history,
I wondered that it could be so hard: after all,
this city had given us our beloved grey steel factory door, our rusty bridges,
          woven impromptu midnight music with passing freight-trains'
          minor-key songs of bygone urban industry;
had let us tumble through our early twenties outsmarting authorities,
          speaking ourselves into being
through smoky, sunlit afternoons like Kerouac characters I loved
and believed in at seventeen. Fortune had granted us eight years
          to play out our formative visions,
          brought to fruition our urban romance,
          this industrial evolution.

FOREIGN DESIGN

For my namesake Sam Cohen (who also made fake nickels)

who had fifteen brothers and sisters   but who knows if all
at one time because how many survived?   One the children
buried in frozen Russian mud somewhere   outside the mud hut
while their parents were in town.

Who crossed the Atlantic Ocean as   a young man, alone,
an eager peasant whose speech   the Ellis Island men
in coats and beards could never   understand and so
when Sam said Kagan, the men   wrote Cohen and thus
gave us a brand new family name.

Who loved Minnie twice his size   in girth, her heavy
black braid drove fair Sam   wild and her
preference was for tall men but   never mind they had
three girls and a store.

Who opened the front door of his   Philadelphia ghetto
home to every scrawny mongrel only   to see them scamper
through the house to his wife   who stood, one hand
on ample hip, the other shooing   those *meshugena hundt*
right out the back door.

Who was not a godfearing man but   was forever getting canned
in the factories for some fellow   who had to piss or
was sick and the bosses would say   Cohen. You don't
wanna make trouble and he didn't,

just thought men should have   the freedom to piss
or speak when they wanted,   though ideas don't
bring home the borscht nor make   flanken more tasty.
Still he learned to speak English   like an American
almost, and rode a motorcycle

with a sidecar for Minnie, and woke   in the night with strange
premonitions which one time saved   my mother's life;
and when not working sat dreaming,   bending ideas into intricate
jewelry he tried to sell under a sign   that read Foregin Desnig.

OUR HOUSE

is a very very very fine house.
We did, for a long time, have two cats but only
very briefly a yard; three different yards. Six
balconies. Always morning glories, purple, periwinkle.
A fireplace, twice. This is your necessity now, to light
the hearth: no new abodes will be
considered unless one can, though who
will place the flowers in the vase? Not
the beloved blue one shattered, held
by glued handle, peonies gone to pieces,
too many to make whole. It showed me almost
nothing, I see now, of Annie, your father's mother
who loved pretty things. So much history a stutter
and I'll never know the word.

I drove my daughter up Spadina today,
shadowy pathway of my infant life, first
red leaves crinkling in the back seat, gathered from the hill
I rolled down as a child. In the woods she said, We're lost; I said
I know the way. You do? (We were far in.) I've been coming here
all my life. The simplicity of this
was new.

In the car, skylight open, I'm in the green
Saab, 1988, year of change (your tape deck daily
intoned *Doors opening doors closing, doors opening doors closing, I am safe,*
it's only change; I liked its tune yet heard
the opposite) – in pursuit of our bucolic
day at Chudleigh's apple orchard, me in braids
and that year's overalls, north to the highway
singing *Our house is a very very very fine house, with two cats in the yard,*
life used to be so hard,
and even then I knew
I was and was not the you
who would make things easy.
So I gathered flowers,
placed them in some vase.

Tonight, across the Sabbath flame,
harvest moon centred in the balcony's frame,
kid songs tinkle in the background
as you happily alight—*the thing*!
You wished to remember
Graham Nash on television, a small concert,
the tale of a pleasant day
with girlfriend Joni Mitchell, an antique shop, nothing fancy,
a pretty vase, and later he said Why don't I
light a fire...

Deer bound over blue flowers
on the cloth laid for autumn;
a flickering meniscus your warm brown eyes:
these two in their ordinary moment
made lasting song? Our house
that only briefly was?
The hearth you cannot find?

My house does not have one.
This was an objection.
But in its orange glow at evening-time,
your old lamp lit on my window-sill
as I see you off, valiant
hobble down the stairs, to your car,
into the dark you must traverse
to the place that is not home (your mother
at my request would open her heavy door
to show my child self The Dark), I turn
towards sleeping babe, the mess of good, full day,
and the warmth of my own hearth burns me.

Our house
is on only two maps.
They do not match,
but superimposed, cross-referenced show
a solid home, the foundation good.
It is generous; rot turns to food.

It houses all I can and cannot know,
is alphabet and song.

If it is dark, and frightening to play there,
one of us lights the fire, and a vase appears,
and sturdy flowers which bloom bright in tears.

SPIT ON THE DEVIL

"Pre-mourning is a form of self-indulgence," says the clever lady
to the frightened mother in *The Fire-Dwellers.*
Fancy speak for get over yourself. The strangest
expression: where shall one get? Into someone
else, I guess, someone smooth as a ladybird's shell,
lacquer meticulous. What if I say it's not myself
that flashes disaster before my eyes? Not me, but blood
imported steerage a century past? Wiring rigged by two bodies
joined in a bed now mine, when one could still receive
a telegram. Your husband dead. Stop. Your child killed. Stop.

If those messages aren't mine, what then my laugh? A flutter
actuated by others, the rustle of trees in wind. Alright.
Perception is a keyhole shaped by unknown hands
through which to witness the process of being;
fear is a screen, grossly ornate,
a hulking heirloom I can't sell or trash,
but which can be stashed in the room's farthest corner.
And love the light it won't disfigure there.

Spit on the Devil, my mother says when I praise
my good fortune, and I stumble into traffic, trip down stairs.
Organs betray me as I sing my love.
If the eye alighting on beauty is weight enough
to crush it, then we must turn our heads aside
and perform this rite, swaddle joy
in winding-sheets. It won't breathe,
but its preciousness will be acknowledged.

Stacey and I, we know better.
Envisioning loss is indulgent
as the blubber encasing our stomachs
after the kids came—not of the self,
but of what can't be helped
in a life too sovereign to collar
with superstition. Don't spit,
it only makes a mess that needs cleaning.

If you believe in things you don't understand
then you suffer...
—Stevie Wonder

SUPERSTITION

The soap opera I've watched
all my life nearly lost me
when they killed off a kid,
spent a whole episode
on the life she should have lived.
Moments before her death
she heard Daddy's soliloquy
on the fearlessness, the bliss
bequeathed him by her smile.

The tawdriness was vile;
worse, its flimsiness
to stifle tears; the ironic tragedy
should have smothered itself—
death by avalanche of garish scarves—
but feeling will breathe beneath the heaviest hand,
vanquish absurdity.

Turns out it's a trope. Any time
characters express the plenitude
of their gratitude: devastation.
Are viewers in the majority prey
to a suspicion, a sneaking superstition
that pride anticipates the fall,
and to rejoice in the face of entropy
is always insolence? Words of love
the blow that shatters the looking-glass,
happiness blue-gold fire, doomed to burn through

the matter that makes it. I, raised
to say *kneina hura* if I say my daughter is healthy,
to spit on the devil if I say my life is good,

have never had a happy moment that wasn't
dogged by fear. Belief
is supposed to make life easier to bear,
but what I wouldn't give to burst
my unwanted faith like a blister,
and all raw and tender touch the world I love.

My thirteen month old child
ignites with glee at the rhythm
of "Superstition" as I try to dance
from my bones the fear every action produces
its equal and opposite reaction,
that each moment of perfection
lights the spark of its destruction;
to believe in the magic I can understand:
the warmth of my darling clasped in my hands.

ON TRANSIENCE

Homes Mom and I dwelled in chart my childhood:
infancy's Lonsdale—dancing to Blondie,
making soups with Mom's scraps in blue plastic
pots. At seven on Marwood, first dog, first
crush, I gave up my soother, and one day
discovered my Mother would die because
if I was getting older so was she.
Pogo stick, blackberry tree, trundle bed:
Grade Three on Vesta; next year Thelma, our
beloved cul-de-sac: Mom quit her job,
recession hit; we bought time with strangers'
change at garage sale after garage sale.
Eleven, I sold my blue kitchen. Grown,
house bought, the scraps still simmer in the pot.

LAYTON, IRVING

I

Out of hubris I pursue you
in the glossy pages of the World Book
Encyclopedia we've had since I was six.

There, below laxative and above
Lazarus, are your three paragraphs:
your life, glossed.

"...), is a Canadian poet.
He writes forceful poems that praise creativity and energy."
(I see your rounded thigh raised in dance like Pan, your moist
closed lids on a face upturned with praise; see the form of your
great grey mane flaming against the sky)
I stand below

my cluttered bookshelves, Post-Structuralism
for Beginners crushed by Childcraft Books, beneath
Hemingway, tattered Kerouac, Austen and your Freud;
there, the L book—number 12—tells me many of your poems
"express the idea
that human beings and nature are identical."
(Do they? I never knew. And you will never see
me on the couch, hair everywhere, agreeing with you)
I realize

I never knew the name
of the town where you were born,
and that now reading it,
I cannot pronounce it.

II

You seem smarter than me.
Then again, when you first published,
you were thirty-three,
the same age my mother was
when she had me.

But how did you acquire your ten trillion words?
How did this knack
for allusion occur?
When did you learn Sagittarius
has 800,000 billion stars?
Or the particulars of so many wars?
I cannot ask you. So,
I read four poems and look up six words.
Two of them are not in my dictionary.

The Encyclopedia does not say
née Israel Lazarovitch, and does not say when
irritated, his eyebrows twitched,
and with gusto he pissed people off.
You influenced verse. You won the Governor-General's.
You were a teacher. The World Book does not
say he tapped fingers counting syllables,
and the perfect mouth kept him awake nights;
nor how some mornings,
tickled with delight
just to be awake
you would do a little dance,
a sweet absurd bounce, like a child who has to pee,
and you'd sing a little song for the new day.

OF WHAT I CAN KNOW

(night scenes on Jackes Avenue)

One of your books lies open
on my knees in the dark apartment.
In the window an image of myself
hangs suspended between high rises.

I imagine you sitting there
in the burgundy chair where my cat lies sleeping.
The few small lights behind you
make a halo of your white hair.

I picture a
kind smile,
a silent assurance.

Soon now, night will fade and you
will be gotten up, your bed made, face washed. Another
day among the ruins, where portraits of you line your walls,
and books whose meanings now elude you.

IT WAS ART

For Nestor Dondoglio

Wrongheaded avenger,
eager fool, I'm glad of the glut of hate in your heart, so much
all the centuries of injustice were cyanide in your hands
as you prepared the rich fucks' banquet.

Your hands,
hardened as they were with your, your friends', your ancestors' lives,
trembled—
trembled revenge, intent, the plot finally in execution,
the hour now come, goose cooked, soup seasoned.

The guests,
bedecked, bejeweled,
blind upon the hangman's stool, sipped at your creation, until
the sounds of retching filled the hall.

What did you think,
seeing your mistake? Your one chance to strike a blow for the revolution,
to feed back the poison of the poisonous rich,
and not one of the bastards dead.

I like to think
that peering 'round the kitchen door
(and years later after final fuckyous
to police and eastward flight) you saw
your gilt-edged night of revolt
robbed of its corpses,
and your failure seemed no failure, but rather deliverance
from murderer to prankster
sublime.

LETTER TO GWENDOLYN BROOKS

About Love... Little can help you. In this matter you are alone, except for your secret and everlasting unfinished acquaintanceship with your own essential needs. But there is one thing I hope you will do: find out if your "choice" is kind—and not just to yourself alone.

— Report from Part One

Mrs. Brooks, it is nice (if I may borrow
a word you liked) to think that I might send
a little epistle to Illinois
asking for some advice. Love, you wrote, is a lonely
endeavor; what we must ask always is
whether the plot we tend will yield
poison or feast. We can never be certain,
must taste, and taste again, and hope each time
to live, learn to know better our systems.
I have a lovely love—have called him so
for years, and daily prune away
bitterness and fear, keep clear the nourishing stem.
And what of that other love, or "choice"—lonelier yet—
for those sweet, meager birds, the ballad, the sonnet?

Langston Hughes in a corner kitchenette
with a hundred friends; early encouragement
from Cullen and Johnson; Lee's incitement
and Fisk university blazing with cold eyes
which opened wide and warm your own,
sparked the canon's moldy fuse. Poetry
is not always a small bird caught in a chimney,
heart pounding narrow corridors of brick and bone.
At first, for you, a key whose intricate twists
you loved, and mastered; later a stone launched
with dozens, among thousands of raised fists;
and ever a generous host to your secret
trysts with your own thoughts. Poems were kindness,
your sane love: a fruitful bean-stalk, sturdy trellis.

The next generation climbed up and saw
it would not do to produce more sonnets,
though their ancestors blazed them like comets
through endless, treacherous atmosphere. Laws
which you had learned and therefore loved, the young
abolished—the whirlwind tore through your known
garden, and you chose to love what was sown;
your pet birds, with their metred tune, you flung
to hands elsewhere. Tonight I wish to ask
how you knew to accept so gracefully
the change from what had been to what might be,
and make strange roots and seeds a fine repast.
Not many are pleased to admit the real
can be the sublime form of the ideal.

If I am captive to a feeble tune
which happens to flutter my days with joy,
or once wake sobbing on my honeymoon
and get no comfort from my lovely boy;
if half of what I grow crumbles to ash,
coats my tongue with the bitter taste of death,
I hope I shall devour the other half
and sing my lovely love with warm sweet breath.
How do we let expectations alter
yet never forsake what we first desire?
Extend our hands to what we most require?
Build not our dreams but days into altars?
If I learn this, poems will be kindness;
I can feed love on this lush loneliness.

Let there be no love poems written
until love can exist freely and
cleanly.

— Amiri Baraka

AND YET, A LOVE POEM

Owls grow in nests of bones,
the remains of prey brought
still kicking.

Our own debt
to death we disavow, how our growth
might be measured in lives devoured.

This page is a dead thing. Its marks
appear without trace of the matter
pillaged for them,

the tired muscles
that chipped the torn earth. I call
my mother. She too is tired.

Love has never been clean,
and is by definition
a bond,

though often
the purest expression
of freedom: for no tyrant

yet has it submit. Virtue's
great virtue? Persistence
amidst iniquity.

A wise
philosopher said to write
poetry after Auschwitz

is barbaric. Yet violence and art
are half-siblings competing
for our attention;

starve one,
the other fattens. If poems too
are assassins, avenging angels

with dagger-language to slice the bowels
from this vicious world,
who will make

the beauty, or
will rage beat the world beautiful?
You, Mr. Baraka, say love poems

have no place in a theater this savage,
cannot staunch the blood from our
botched operation.

This is almost true.
No desire or act of love can
wash clean our colosseum.

May no one miss the vigilant brutality
that triggered your wrathful words.
I have not suffered

with you, I am
safe here in my brick house.
My child could play with a water gun.

How can we speak, though, without echoing
off the bones that house us,
their imprint indelible

as an umbilicus? What if
all poems speak love, are a recognition
of the world in all its malignant beauty.

If Mandelstam could write *I love*
my poor earth because I have
seen no other,

while waiting
for his bullet, saying goodbye
every day for most of his life,

I cannot renounce love, withhold
forgiveness, demand this world
be other than it is

before I praise it.
If we dream clean, free dreams
those are surely love poems;

prayers, protests, angry conversations too
are poetry, invocations of the world
as we wish it to be.

So tells me
the boy I love, truest soul,
my solitary twin;

each day I wake to look at
him counters the terror of Eichmann,
Stalin, Rumsfeld, Netanyahu, the Klan,

and the mad crownless princes
one might be tempted to menace
were revolution upon us.

There is, alas,
no universe next door
except your neighbor.

I wish to have him enter
my corner of this nest,
this warm grave

in which we all
are raised; be together wide-eyed
indignant children, touch the bones

like notes, play upon this
rude, filthy xylophone
love songs for the world.

AFTER THE WEDDING

I

As we tumble into the car
outside the happy tumult of your cousin's wedding
your mom sharing my smoke tells me about the times
when your grandfather would polka, polka
champion he used to dance her
three inches above ground.

II

I watch your father's strong, veined
hands on the wheel,
wife quiet beside him
calm in the close darkness.
I think about men
resisting and desisting.

III

My hand above your ear
I try to hold still
your head as it knocks an uneven beat
into my collarbone, my cheek
to your swirling crown.

IV

The high beams cut a brief path:
pebbles and dust, our ghostly companions,
dance and cling.
I think you are one third of
the way through your life.

V

Our time is
trapped in an accordion
collapsed, breathless, and we
are dancing a merciless two-step
toward old flesh and forgetfulness,
grown children and frightening nights,
the corridor of life
passed through. All I want
is to arrive and have to wake you,
see you stretch your young bones
and say hello

IN MEMORIAM: A LETTER

My bible tells me that Good Friday comes before Easter.
And I have not lost faith, I'm not in despair. I haven't lost faith
because I know that the arc of the universe is long,
but it bends toward justice.

— Dr. Martin Luther King

Dr. King, you were disappointed with America.
You saw the horrors of its wars, knew the
causes. You called them out. Like a good father
whose smart child does a stupid thing, you
expected more, asked for it by loving. Of course
a country is not a son, countries have other,
simpler ways to dispatch obstacles. More complete.
Guilt is so light dispersed amongst many.
You would say, I suppose, I shouldn't be bitter:
My bible tells me that Good Friday comes before Easter.

Dr. King, you saw freedom rise, people willing
to die for it. Sundays your church must have
overflowed with those who believed your proclamation:
Out of the wounds of a frail new world, new systems
of justice and equality are being born.
But they were stillborn, Dr. King. Your wraith
and theirs haunt the nation, illuminate
these dark hours of history, when Beauty has all been bought,
Love sold, and God has died, intestate.
And I have not lost faith, I'm not in despair. I haven't lost faith

yet daily I lose faith, lose heart. To mark the first
day of this year, my friends gathered, and aimless,
tired, sunk in a guilty ennui, we let your sermon rouse us.
Reverend Dr. King, religion is to me as some half-sibling gone wicked,
in whose bad deeds are manifested all my secret flaws,
and faith the siren's voice that leads his weak mind wrong.
Yet when you preach, half a century collapses, I am calling
amen with your congregation. From you I might learn how to struggle
gracefully, learn to whistle a nightingale's song
because I know that the arc of the universe is long

and my lifetime short. That is a comfort. Dr. King,
I am alright with unfinished business
and *walking the streets with a burdened heart*
some days. You were right. To try is enough,
to love, in spite of reasons not to love.
If I must believe something then I will believe this:
humanity is a great tree that reaches out into a dark sky,
memories of millennia stored in its trunk; it grows
heedlessly, without purpose,
but it bends toward justice.

DEAR READER

1

Since I began to collect my thoughts
far back in the early aughts,
much has changed. Tim Horton's
features gay sweethearts in an ad run
in the Oscars; Canadian Tire
a vignette of the desire
to include, to equalize.
And at the great pageant itself—surprise!
The award goes not to a fantasy
of dreams realized, but the reality
of striving just to be seen,
to be. We liberals are so keen
these days to demonstrate
we care, as if to compensate
for all the wrongs we've failed to right,
as if to bring our faults to light
ourselves, like Austen's Emma, first –
before it's done by someone we've hurt
(we're quite magnificently late).

Michael is sweeping; I sponge
things; we're listening
to a podcast: Washington
Foreign Policy wonks (my newsman
explains) giving their takes.
The Middle East is a game
of Jenga, one says, then: *Evaluate*
my metaphor, his voice
amused. (Which really
they must; that being his move,
it advances the game
in a certain manner.) Another
notes the phrase *foreign policy engagements*
ennobles the activity; someone demands
redefine coward.

Their speech might turn flesh
to dust (what entity transforms
metaphor to drone?)—thus
I am surprised, impressed
by their attentiveness
to words, their tacit admission
the yarn affects the pattern.

2

In the mud-room, piled
with refuse, smoking
my almost last again. Idiot
symbol of brazenness, as if
to deny the difference
between odds and chance,
like a charm of the thing feared
keeps it from the door.

Sonnet, the new insurance company
advises: *protect your optimism,*
shows a candle lit in the rain. Hari
Nef is a gorgeous L'Oreal vision,
surely a good sign that the day is nigh
when we stop discussing pronouns, bathrooms
(great symbol of our age: the glorified
holes where we void our waste.) When we consume
the proffered things that make us feel ourselves
progressing, do we build the world we wish,
or gild our rot and think we have done well?
Does the greeting card contain the message?
No. Yet we can't say what we can't envisage.

It seems that whenever we celebrate
we're always too early, or much too late.
Exhume those bodies! the actress cries
as she accepts her well-earned prize

for bringing to the silver screen
an avatar of many who have been
and are alive, if in new clothes. And when
they wheel on-stage a real-life heroine,
she gets a standing o! (In the film
about her life, a potent emblem
of racial strife is a distant bathroom
whose sign a white man delivers to doom.)
We have exhumed! Given speech and dress
to those who suffered, let them sing of our progress
into a world where we know what we did,
if not what we do, and deem it wretched.

3

But this is harsh. We have to know,
must devise rites
by which to show
what we can't see. *No one*
hates a photojournalist, Michael says;
and to my protest (If a child is on fire
?): *That question comes*
later; at least no one says that they lie,
or skew.

This may be true.
Even so, we can't transmute
event to knowledge,
only transmit. All languages
our little Ouija boards through which we're forced
to conjure one another, past and present – each of us
a bone planchette
seeking the right letters.

Often we find them. My mother
attended a shiva for her
first husband, a comedian—
meta before that was a word,
his best friend described his art—and

somehow the warm, full room conjured
the sweetness of the buried one:
clink of cups, requisite platters
of cream cheese and smoked salmon
nourished the forms they served. Laughter,
songs, well-tended tales—thought tickling air—
distill, and bring the distant near
enough to feel, if not to touch;
and this is something, if not much.

4

The news again. The White House and the Kremlin
both deploy the terms *fake news, witch hunt*
to deny possible ties; our
handsome PM firmly grips, drops
the new leader's hand, sparks many memes;
a new study shows mercury levels too high
in Grassy Narrows—wait, new study?

Shall we stay up late and talk? Shall we
meet and walk and look at all the things
the world has built or blundered?

We might not, for days
go fast, and we may
lack the right maps; still,
I wish to know. Do your days involve
careful selection of emojis? (Mine do, surprisingly.) What
do you love to watch or read? Have for dinner? What's the best
world you can see? (Right now, any one
where I'm not talking? Sorry—almost through!
Or shut the gate—I appreciate
your querying who called!)

There's a debate on: rudeness or politeness: be it resolved
we need more of each. What do you say? Or to the scholar
twice on the radio this week? He contends,
of virtual reality, its social promise:

Empathy leads us morally astray...
It gets weaponized...

I might imagine myself in your life,
or simply know you are alive,
wish you to thrive for that reason.
How shall we give love its definition?

ACKNOWLEDGEMENTS:

Thanks first to Denis De Klerck for the opportunity to turn these poems into a book, and for insightful edits. Thanks to Priscila Uppal, under whose tutelage some of these poems were first workshopped and whose kindness and support are deeply appreciated. Thanks to Richard Teleky, Susan Swan, and to every person in York's Creative Writing program 2002-2005. To Molly Peacock, for her expertise; to Robert Priest, Vanessa Shields and David Goldstein for being early readers. To Thomas Loebel for understanding and the word "relation"; Karen Valihora, for showing me how it's done. To David Layton, for being my brother, and immense fun. To Uncle Marc, for love and the zaniest emails; Franceszka Koletacz (Auntie Broom) and family, for family; and to Janice and Brian Bobbie and Sheila Allen for love and support. To Shira Leuchter and family, Tova Kardonne, Leslie Barnes, and every one of my friends who make life rich and good: our time together is woven through these pages. To the "dissertation group"—Dani Spinoza, Melissa Dalgleish, Thom Bryce, and Jonathan Vandor, for clarifying ideas and clogging arteries, and to everyone who has made my time in York's Graduate English program so valuable and fun. To Itay Keshet, for Eastern Avenue and all it made; Elinor Keshet, for reaching out; Jamie Smith, for love and ideas; Jake Wadland, for the harshest critiques and kindest friendship; Ariel Garten, for making things and asking me to; Florence Shaw, for marvelous characters; Bri Sharpe, for singing with me. To the teachers at Northern Secondary 1994-1998 who made high school a breeding ground for ideas and relationships. To Helena Likwornik, whose irrepressible giggle teaches me we are more than the sum of our parts. To my ancestors, for being. Special thanks to Eshe Mercer-James, for reading everything, for growing up with me, for safety; and to Dave Arcus and Bouks, for art and joy. To Joseph Clark, who makes me want to write, for stillness, clarity, beauty. Most loving and humble thanks to my mom, Harriet, my first reader always, for a lifetime of encouragement, for being the greatest Bubbie, for saving and marking things I should read, for teaching me to debate and the meaning of love. Thank you, Michael Bobbie. Without you none of this would exist: these ideas, the time to express them, the joy that enables them, our daughter and all that wonder —you make all my wishes reality, ptu ptu ptu... But fuck that nonsense, what I've said is simply true, a fact you've taught me to feel.

"Eulogy for Finn" and "Happiness" originally appeared in *The Fiddlehead*; "In Memoriam: A Letter" in *Here We Are Among the Living* (Tightrope, 2012); "Spit on the Devil," "Superstition," "Epithalamion," "It Was Art," and "To the Allen Expressway" in *The White Wall Review*; "Song for Ida," "The First Month," "After the Wedding" "Rummy" "High School Choir Director" and "Zees" in *The Windsor Review*; "Olga" and "Layton, Irving" in *Studio*; "Industrial Evolution (A Reprise)," "Sonnets for the Flower-Men," and "To Toronto" in *TOK 3: Writing the New Toronto* (Zephyr, 2008); "Layton, Irving" and "Of What I Can Know" in *Exile*.

Samantha Bernstein is a Toronto writer and a PhD candidate at York University. Her first book, the memoir, *Here We Are Among The Living* was nominated for a B.C. National Award for Nonfiction. Her poetry has appeared in *Exile*, The *Fiddlehead Literary Journal*, and on the *Toronto Poetry Map*, among other places and she was featured in Sook Yin Lee's documentary *Where Have All The Poets Gone?* discussing the influence of her father, the legendary poet Irving Layton.